To Love and To Marry

To Love
and
To Marry

BEAUTIFUL TRIBUTES

TO LOVE AND MARRIAGE

SELECTED BY MARIANNE WILSON

ILLUSTRATED BY GLORIA NIXON

HALLMARK CROWN EDITIONS

To Love and To Marry

When the wedding march sounds

the resolute approach,

the clock no longer ticks;

it tolls the hour . . . .

The figures in the aisle

are no longer individuals;

they symbolize the human race.

ANNE MORROW LINDBERGH

I Wish I Could Remember
That First Day ·

I wish I could remember that first day,
First hour, first moment of your meeting me,
If bright or dim the season, it might be
Summer or winter for aught I can say;
So unrecorded did it slip away,
So blind was I to see and to foresee,
So dull to mark the budding of my tree
That would not blossom yet for many a May.
If only I could recollect it, such
A day of days! I let it come and go
As traceless as a thaw of bygone snow;
It seemed to mean so little, meant so much;
If only now I could recall that touch,
First touch of hand in hand—did one but know!

Christina Rossetti

The aspiration of lovers: to be as necessary to each
other as the World to God, and God to the World.

Richard Garnett

6

Shall I Compare Thee
To A Summer's Day?

Shall I compare thee to a summer's day?
Thou art more lovely and more temperate.
Rough winds do shake the darling buds of May,
And summer's lease hath all too short a date:
Sometime too hot the eye of heaven shines,
And often is his gold complexion dimmed;
And every fair from fair sometime declines,
By chance or nature's changing course untrimmed;
But thy eternal summer shall not fade,
Nor lose possession of that fair thou owest;
Nor shall Death brag thou wander'st in his shade,
When in eternal lines to time thou grow'st.
   So long as men can breathe, or eyes can see,
   So long lives this, and this gives life to thee.

William Shakespeare

An eternal hunger for love and beauty is my desire;
I know now that those who possess bounty alone are
naught but miserable, but to my spirit the sighs of
lovers are more soothing than music of the lyre.

Kahlil Gibran

How Do I Love Thee?

How do I love thee? Let me count the ways.
I love thee to the depth and breadth and height
My soul can reach, when feeling out of sight
For the ends of Being and Ideal Grace.
I love thee to the level of every day's
Most quiet need, by sun and candlelight.
I love thee freely, as men strive for Right;
I love thee purely, as they turn from Praise;
I love thee with the passion put to use
In my old griefs, and with my childhood's faith;
I love thee with a love I seemed to lose
With my lost saints,—I love thee with the breath,
Smiles, tears, of all my life!—and, if God choose,
I shall but love thee better after death.

Elizabeth Barrett Browning

Romance

I will make you brooches and toys for your delight
Of bird-song at morning and star-shine at night.
I will make a palace fit for you and me
Of green days in forests and blue days at sea.

I will make my kitchen and you shall keep your room
Where white flows the river and bright blows the broom,
And you shall wash your linen and keep your body white
In rainfall at morning and dewfall at night.

And this shall be for music when no one else is near,
The fine song for singing, the rare song to hear!
That only I remember, that only you admire,
Of the broad road that stretches and the roadside fire.

Robert Louis Stevenson

Love is the enchanted dawn of every heart.

Lamartine

Love is a circle, that doth restless move
In the same sweet eternity of love.   *Robert Herrick*

Rain

I have always hated the rain,
And the gloom of grayed skies.
But now I think I must always cherish
Rain-hung leaf and the misty river;
And the friendly screen of dripping green
Where eager kisses were shyly given
And your pipe-smoke made clouds in our damp,
    close heaven.

The curious laggard passed us by,
His wet shoes soughed on the shining walk.
And that afternoon was filled with a blurred glory—
That afternoon, when we first talked as lovers.

Jean Starr Untermeyer

To Dianeme

Give me one kiss,   To enrich you,
And no more;   I'll restore
If so be, this   For that one, two
Makes you poor;   Thousand score.

Robert Herrick

Brown Penny

I whispered, "I am too young."
And then, "I am old enough";
Wherefore I threw a penny
To find out if I might love.
"Go and love, go and love, young man,
If the lady be young and fair."
Ah, penny, brown penny, brown penny,
I am looped in the loops of her hair.
O love is the crooked thing,
There is nobody wise enough
To find out all that is in it,
For he would be thinking of love
Till the stars had run away,
And the shadows eaten the moon.
Ah, penny, brown penny, brown penny,
One cannot begin it too soon.

William Butler Yeats

Never marry but for love, but see that thou lovest
what is lovely.   *William Penn*

Lovers' Infiniteness

If yet I have not all thy love,
Dear, I shall never have it all.
I cannot breathe one other sigh to move,
Nor can entreat one other tear to fall,
And all my treasure, which should purchase thee—
Sighs, tears, and oaths, and letters—I have spent.
Yet no more can be due to me
Than at the bargain made was meant.
If then thy gift of love were partial,
That some to me, some should to others fall,
　Dear, I shall never have thee all.

Or if then thou gavest me all,
All was but all which thou hadst then;
But if in thy heart, since, there be or shall,
New love created be, by other men,
Which have their stocks entire, and can in tears,
In sighs, in oaths, and letters outbid me,
This new love was not vowed by thee.
And yet it was, thy gift being general:
The ground, thy heart, is mine, whatever shall
　Grow there, Dear, I should have it all.

Yet I would not have all yet.
He that hath all can have no more,
And since my love doth every day admit
New growth, thou shouldst have new rewards
    in store;
Thou canst not every day give me thy heart;
If thou canst give it, then thou never gavest it:
Love's riddles are, that though thy heart depart,
It stays at home, and thou with losing savest it:
But we will have a way more liberal
Than changing hearts: to join them, so we shall
    Be one, and one another's All.

John Donne

*L*ove vanquishes time. To lovers, a moment can be
eternity, eternity can be the tick of a clock. Across the
barriers of time and the ultimate destiny, love persists,
for the home of the beloved, absent or present, is always
in the mind and heart. Absence does not diminish love.

Mary Parrish

For Those Who Love

Time is ...

   Too slow for those who wait,

Too swift for those who fear,

   Too long for those who grieve,

      Too short for those who rejoice;

But for those who love,

   Time is not.

HENRY VAN DYKE

For Miriam

Do I not deal with angels
When her lips I touch

So gentle, so warm and sweet—falsity
Has no sight of her
O the world is a place of veils and roses
When she is there

I am come to her wonder
Like a boy finding a star in a haymow
And there is nothing cruel or mad or evil
Anywhere

Kenneth Patchen

Man can live his truth, his deepest truth, but cannot
speak it. It is for this reason that love becomes
the ultimate human answer to the ultimate human question.

Archibald MacLeish

The Voice of My Beloved

The voice of my beloved!
   Behold, he comes,
leaping upon the mountains,
   bounding over the hills.
My beloved is like a gazelle,
   or a young stag.
Behold, there he stands
   behind our wall,
gazing in at the windows,
   looking through the lattice.
My beloved speaks and says to me:
"Arise, my love, my fair one,
   and come away;
for lo, the winter is past,
   the rain is over and gone.
The flowers appear on the earth,
   the time of singing has come,
and the voice of the turtledove
   is heard in our land.
The fig tree puts forth its figs,
   and the vines are in blossom;
   they give forth fragrance.
Arise, my love, my fair one,
   and come away . . . ."

Song of Solomon 2:8-13 (RSVB)

She Walks in Beauty

She walks in beauty like the night
Of cloudless climes and starry skies;
And all that's best of dark and bright
Meets in her aspect and her eyes:
Thus mellow'd to that tender light
Which heaven to gaudy day denies.

One shade the more, one ray the less,
Had half impair'd the nameless grace
Which waves in every raven tress,
Or softly lightens o'er her face—
Where thoughts serenely sweet express
How pure, how dear their dwelling-place.

And on that cheek, and o'er that brow,
So soft, so calm, yet eloquent,
The smiles that win, the tints that glow,
But tell of days in goodness spent,
A mind at peace with all below,
A heart whose love is innocent.

George Gordon, Lord Byron

*A*thing of beauty is a joy forever.   *John Keats*

The Bridesmaid

O bridesmaid, ere the happy knot was tied,
Thine eyes so wept that they could hardly see;
Thy sister smiled and said, "No tears for me!
A happy bridesmaid makes a happy bride."
And then, the couple standing side by side,
Love lighted down between them full of glee,
And over his left shoulder laugh'd at thee,
"O happy bridesmaid, make a happy bride."
And all at once a pleasant truth I learned,
For while the tender service made thee weep,
I loved thee for the tear thou couldst not hide,
And prest thy hand and knew the press returned,
And thought, "My life is sick of single sleep:
O happy bridesmaid, make a happy bride."

Alfred, Lord Tennyson

There is nothing enduring in life for a woman except
what she builds in a man's heart.   *Judith Anderson*

From 'The Bells'

Hear the mellow wedding bells,—Golden bells!
What a world of happiness their harmony foretells!
Through the balmy air of night
How they ring out their delight!
From the molten golden notes,
What a liquid ditty floats
To the turtle-dove that listens,
   while she gloats on the moon!
Oh, from out the sounding cells,
What a gush of euphony voluminously wells!
  How it swells!
    How it dwells
On the Future! How it tells
Of the rapture that impels
To the swinging and the ringing
Of the bells, bells, bells,
Of the bells, bells, bells, bells,
  Bells, bells, bells,—
To the rhyming and the chiming of the bells!

Edgar Allan Poe

My Delight and Thy Delight

My delight and thy delight
Walking, like two angels white,
In the gardens of the night:

My desire and thy desire
Twining to a tongue of fire,
Leaping live, and laughing higher:

Thro' the everlasting strife
In the mystery of life.
Love, from whom the world begun,
Hath the secret of the sun.

Love can tell, and love alone,
Whence the million stars were strewn,
Why each atom knows its own,
How, in spite of woe and death,
Gay is life, and sweet is breath:

This he taught us, this we knew,
Happy is his science true,
Hand in hand as we stood
'Neath the shadows of the wood,
Heart to heart as we lay
In the dawning of the day.

Robert Bridges

The Night Before Marriage

Tomorrow, when I come to you,
   I put within your hand
Body and heart and soul, as who
   but women understand?

My lover, make me wholly yours
   in all the ways there are,
So a sweet bondage more endures
   than either lock or bar;

So that I never leave your breast
   to dream of other things,
But find in you my end-of-quest,
   my comfort . . . and my wings.

Florence Jacobs

Therefore shall a man leave his father and his mother, and shall cleave unto his wife: and they shall be one flesh.   *Genesis 2:24*

The Story of the Bridal Veil

When Abraham was far advanced in years he sent his
most trusted servant to Mesopotamia to find a wife
for his son, Isaac. With ten camels and many gifts—
silver, gold, and raiment—the servant arrived at his
destination. Tired and thirsty from his journey,
he approached a well, where he saw a comely young
woman. Her name was Rebecca.

As the servant came near, Rebecca covered her face
with her veil, as was the custom among women of virtue.
He asked her for water and she answered, "Drink and
I will give your camels drink also." These words were
the sign that the servant had prayed to God for. They
told him this was the woman who should be Isaac's wife.

The servant explained his mission to Rebecca, and she
urged him to see Bethuel, her father. When Bethuel
had heard the servant's words, he said it was the Lord's
will that Rebecca go to Isaac. Gifts were given to the
family, and Rebecca and the servant left on the journey
back.

Isaac was in the fields when Rebecca and the servant
approached. Rebecca saw Isaac, and immediately alighted
from her camel. She removed her veil, and went to
Isaac, and he took her into his home. They became husband and wife.

Through history the bridal veil has been worn as
Rebecca wore her veil. In the act of removing it,
the bride tells her groom that she has given herself
to him for life.   *Based on The Book of Genesis*

A Wedding Tradition

Something Old . . .
Wear something old, from a bygone year
Which, like your love, is lasting and dear.

Something New . . .
Wear something new as a token, too,
Of the wonderful life that's beginning for you.

Something Borrowed . . .
Wear something borrowed and it will tell
That friends and loved ones wish you well.

Something Blue . . .
Wear something blue, like the skies above
When two hearts enter a world of love.

And a Penny, Too . . .
And place a penny inside your shoe
To assure good fortune your whole lives through.

Barbara Burrow

Oblation

Oh, how my body blooms from every vein,
more fragrant, since you came into my ken.
See how I walk, more slender and upright,
and you wait calmly—and who are you, then?

Behold: I feel that I have left me far
behind and shed my old life, leaf by leaf,
till finally there is nothing but the star
of your smile shining richly on our life.

Everything that through my childhood years
was nameless still and glistening like water
I will christen after you before the altar,
which is made radiant by your shining hair,
the altar which your breasts have lightly crowned.

> *Rainer Maria Rilke*
> *(Tr.C.F. MacIntyre)*

This is now bone of my bones, and flesh of my flesh.

> *Genesis 2:23*

Love's Philosophy

The fountains mingle with the river
And the rivers with the ocean,
The winds of heaven mix forever
With a sweet emotion;
Nothing in the world is single,
All things by a law divine
In one another's being mingle—
Why not I with thine?

See the mountains kiss high heaven,
And the waves clasp one another;
No sister-flower would be forgiven
If it disdain'd its brother;
And the sunlight clasps the earth,
And the moonbeams kiss the sea—
What are all these kissings worth,
If thou kiss not me?

Percy Bysshe Shelley

*L*ove makes all hard hearts gentle.   *Old Proverb*

The Bride

As slim and straight as the candles at her side
She stands, a flower with a flower's own grace.
Sheathed in the petaled satin of a bride,
Wrapped in a shimmering mist of fragile lace,
Serious and shy and very sweet,
She waits her lover's coming, eyes abrim
With happy dreams that are not yet complete
And only can be realized through him.

Here on the threshold of the years she stands,
So soon to leave her girlhood in the past.
God give her lover tender heart and hands
That the white radiance in her eyes may last;
God give her wisdom that she, too, may hold
His love till all the fires of earth grow cold.

Grace Noll Crowell

It is difficult to define love. But we may say that
in the soul, it is a ruling passion; in the mind, it
is a close sympathy and affinity; in the body, a wholly
secret and delicate longing to possess what we love—
and this after much mystery.

La Rochefoucauld

To Be Womanly

To be womanly is to be loving. To be happy is to
be given the opportunity to express that love. To
be blessed is to have love returned. Love is not
what you think. It does what mind cannot do, it
goes where mind cannot follow. Its nature is
transcendental and when we love we at once trans-
cend ourselves and are most ourselves. This is the
way man conceives God, and woman feels that in
truly loving she is nearest heaven.

Jessamyn West

Love Song

Sweep the house clean,
hang fresh curtains
in the windows
put on a new dress
and come with me!

The elm is scattering
its little loaves
of sweet smells
from a white sky!

Who shall hear of us
in the time to come?
Let him say there was
a burst of fragrance
from black branches.

William Carlos Williams

Wedding Prayer

O Father, our hearts are filled with great happiness.
This is our wedding day. We come before you at the
altar of love, pledging our lives and our hearts to
one another.

Grant that we may be ever true and loving, living
together in such a way as to never bring shame or heart-
break into our marriage. Temper our hearts with kind-
ness and understanding and rid them of all pretense or
jealousy.

Help us to be sweetheart, helpmate, friend and guide,
and together, may we meet the cares and problems of life
more bravely. And as time takes away our youthful charm,
may we find contentment in the greater joy of rich
companionship.

May our home truly be a place of love and harmony
where your Spirit is ever present.

Bless our wedding day, we pray, and walk beside us,
Father, through all our life together.   Amen

Mary Dawson Hughes

Nuptial love maketh mankind, friendly love
      perfecteth it . . . .   *Francis Bacon*

To Have and To Hold

To have and to hold

    From this day forward,

For better for worse,

    For richer for poorer,

In sickness and in health,

To love and to cherish,

    Till death do us part.

BOOK OF COMMON PRAYER, 1662

Poem in Prose

This poem is for my wife
I have made it plainly and honestly
The mark is on it
Like the burl on the knife

I have not made it for praise
She has no more need for praise
Than summer has
On the bright days

In all that becomes a woman
Her words and her ways are beautiful
Love's lovely duty
The well-swept room

Wherever she is there is sun
And time and a sweet air
Peace is there
Work done

There are always curtains and flowers
And candles and baked bread
And a cloth spread
And a clean house

Her voice when she sings is a voice
At dawn by a freshening sea
Where the wave leaps in the
Wind and rejoices

Wherever she is it is now
It is here where the apples are
Here in the stars
In the quick hour

The greatest and richest good—
My own life to live—
This she has given me

If giver could

Archibald MacLeish

L ove has the power to give in a moment
what toil can scarcely reach in an age.
Goethe

To My Dear and Loving Husband

If ever two were one, then surely we.
If ever man were lov'd by wife, then thee.
If ever wife was happy in a man,
Compare with me, ye women, if you can.
I prize thy love more than whole mines of gold,
Or all the riches that the East doth hold.
My love is such that rivers cannot quench,
Nor ought but love from thee give recompense.
Thy love is such I can no way repay;
The heavens reward thee manifold I pray.
Then while we live, in love let's so persevere,
That when we live no more, we may live ever.

Anne Bradstreet

It is the man and woman united that makes the complete
human being. Separate she lacks his force of body and
strength of reason; he her softness, sensibility and
acute discernment. Together they are most likely to
succeed in the world. *Benjamin Franklin*

The Legend of the Orange Blossoms

When the conquering Roman legions entered Portugal
in the 3rd century, a marriage was arranged between
the victorious Roman General and a beautiful princess of the Portuguese royal family. He had loved
her ever since he first heard stories of her beauty
and charm. Although she admired him, the Princess
also feared him because of the stories she had heard
of his fierceness in battle.

At a sumptuous banquet before the wedding, the bride
and groom saw one another for the first time. But
silence came between them—a silence of awe on her
part and a silence of love on his. After the banquet,
the General walked alone across the Palace grounds to
his encampment.

"How beautiful she is," he thought. "If only I
could drive the fear from her eyes and let her know
that I would love her tenderly all our lives."

As he walked, he found himself in a garden of small
orange trees. "How fragrant they are! Like the per-
fume in her hair. And purest white, like her own pure
soul."

Prompted by these thoughts, he gathered a spray of
the lovely orange blossoms and sent them by messenger
to the Princess. She was so touched by this tender
gift from the great soldier that she shyly joined him
in the garden. Soon they were walking hand in hand
among the orange blossoms, and in her heart a quiet
love grew that matched his own.

On their wedding day the Princess carried a spray
of orange blossoms. Since that time these white flowers,
a symbol of deepest love, have been carried by brides
everywhere.

For Every Bride

For every bride who walks with shining faith
Into the day new promise has begun;
I'd ask not castles reaching to the sun
Nor golden doors to smug security,
But only this . . .
May love have kept for her,
When twenty other years have come and gone,
The wonder of the rose and purple dawn,
The thrill in every bud that heralds spring,
The peace of evening lights in twilight skies,
The joy of rain upon the thirsty grass . . .
And dreams to challenge all the years that pass
To dim that star today lights in her eyes.

Dixie Willson

A Decade

When you came, you were like red wine and honey,
And the taste of you burnt my mouth with its sweetness.
Now you are like morning bread,
Smooth and pleasant.
I hardly taste you at all, for I know your savor;
But I am completely nourished.

Amy Lowell

To His Love

An old silver church in a forest
Is my love for you.
The trees around it
Are words that I have stolen from your heart.
An old silver bell, the last smile you gave,
Hangs at the top of my church.
It rings only when you come through the forest
And stand beside it.
And then it has no need for ringing,
For your voice takes its place.

Maxwell Bodenheim

It is by loving and not by being loved that one can
come nearest the soul of another; yea, where two love
it is the loving of each other, and not the being loved
by each other, that originates the perfects and
ensures their blessedness.   *George MacDonald*

She Rose To His Requirement

She rose to his requirement—dropped
The playthings of her life
To take the honorable work
Of woman and of wife.

If aught she missed in her new day
Of amplitude—or awe—
Or first prospective—or the gold
In using wore away—

It lay unmentioned—as the sea
Develops pearl and weed—
But only to himself is known
The fathoms they abide.

Emily Dickinson

Kind is my love today, tomorrow kind,
Still constant in a wondrous excellence.

William Shakespeare

Dear, If You Change

Dear, if you change, I'll never choose again,
Sweet, if you shrink, I'll never think of love;
Fair, if you fail, I'll judge all beauty vain,
Wise, if too weak, my wits I'll never prove.
   Dear, sweet, fair, wise; change, shrink
     and be not weak,
   And on my faith, my faith shall never break.

Earth with her flowers shall sooner heav'n adorn,
Heaven her bright stars through earth's dim
   globe shall move,
Fire's heat shall loose and frosts of
   flames be borne,
Air made to shine as black as hell shall prove:
   Earth, heaven, fire, air, the world
     transform'd shall view,
  Ere I prove false to faith, or strange to you.

Old English Air

All mankind love a lover.   *Ralph Waldo Emerson*

My Heart Has Its Love

The sea has its pearls,

The heaven its stars—

But my heart, my heart,

My heart has its love!

HEINRICH HEINE

They Call Her Blessed

A good wife who can find?
  She is far more precious than
    jewels.
The heart of her husband trusts in
    her,
  and he will have no lack of gain.
She does him good, and not harm,
  all the days of her life.
She seeks wool and flax,
  and works with willing hands.
She is like the ships of the merchant,
  she brings her food from afar.
She rises while it is yet night
  and provides food for her household
    and tasks for her maidens.
She considers a field and buys it;
  with the fruit of her hands she
    plants a vineyard.
She girds her loins with strength
    and makes her arms strong.
She perceives that her merchandise
    is profitable.
  Her lamp does not go out at night.
She puts her hands to the distaff,
  and her hands hold the spindle.
She opens her hand to the poor,
  and reaches out her hands to the
    needy.
She is not afraid of snow for her
    household,
  for all her household are clothed
    in scarlet.

She makes herself coverings;
    her clothing is fine linen and
        purple.
Her husband is known in the gates,
    when he sits among the elders of
        the land.
She makes linen garments and sells
        them;
    she delivers girdles to the merchant.
Strength and dignity are her clothing,
    and she laughs at the time to
        come.
She opens her mouth with wisdom,
    and the teaching of kindness is
        on her tongue.
She looks well to the ways of her
        household,
    and does not eat the bread of
        idleness.
Her children rise up and call her blessed;
    her husband also, and he praises
        her:
"Many women have done excellently,
    but you surpass them all."
Charm is deceitful, and beauty is vain,
    but a woman who fears the Lord
        is to be praised.
Give her of the fruit of her hands,
    and let her works praise her in
        the gates.

Proverbs 31:10-31 (RSVB)

House of Dreams

You took my empty dreams
  And filled them every one
With tenderness and nobleness,
  April and the sun.

The old empty dreams
  Where my thoughts would throng
Are far too full of happiness
  To even hold a song.

Oh, the empty dreams were dim
  And the empty dreams were wide,
They were sweet and shadowy houses
  Where my thoughts could hide.

But you took my dreams away
  And you made them all come true—
My thoughts have no place now to play,
  And nothing now to do.

Sara Teasdale

Believe Me,
If All Those Endearing Young Charms

Believe me, if all those endearing young charms,
Which I gaze on so fondly today,
Were to change by tomorrow, and fleet
   in my arms,
Like fairy-gifts fading away,
Thou wouldst still be adored, as this moment
   thou art,
Let thy loveliness fade as it will,
And around the dear ruin each wish of my heart
Would entwine itself verdantly still.

It is not while beauty and youth are thine own,
And thy cheeks unprofaned by a tear,
That the fervor and faith of a soul may be known,
To which time will but make thee more dear!
No, the heart that has truly loved never forgets,
But as truly loves on to the close,
As the sunflower turns to her god when he sets
The same look which she turned when he rose!

Thomas Moore

Hail, wedded love! mysterious law,
        true source
Of human offspring, sole propriety,
In Paradise of all things common else.   *John Milton*

The Art of Marriage

The whole art of marriage lies in the ability to pass
from love to friendship without sacrificing love. It
is not utterly impossible. The white heat of passion
sometimes burns to the very end, but where husband and
wife are really one, "that magnificent silk, so richly
embroidered, is lined with another, simpler, but of
so rare and fine a texture that one is tempted to
prefer it to what covers it." The dominant note, then,
is one of confidence, whose perfection is matched by
the degree of mutual understanding which goes with it
and an affection so watchful that it foresees the
reactions of the beloved.   *André Maurois*

*L*et your task be to render yourself worthy of love and
this even more for your own happiness than for that
of another.   *Maurice Maeterlinck*

This is the true measure of love,

When we believe

That we alone can love,

That no one could ever have

Loved so before us,

That no one will ever love

In the same way after us.

GOETHE

My Love Comes Walking

My love comes walking,
And these flowers
That never saw her 'til this day
Look up; but then
Bend down straightway.

My love sees nothing here but me,
Who never trembled thus before;
And glances down
Lest I do more.

My love is laughing;
Those wild things
Were never tame until I too,
Down-dropping, kissed
Her silvery shoe.

Mark Van Doren

*L*ove is ever the beginning of Knowledge,
as fire is of light.   *Thomas Carlyle*

An Immorality

Sing we for love and idleness,
Naught else is worth the having.

Though I have been in many a land,
There is naught else in living.

And I would rather have my sweet,
Though rose-leaves die of grieving,

Than do high deeds in Hungary
To pass all men's believing.

Ezra Pound

L ove is an endless forgiveness, a tender look
which becomes a habit.   *Peter Ustinov*

G od, the best maker of all marriages,
    Combine your hearts in one.
                    William Shakespeare

This Precious Treasure

The treasures of the deep are not so precious
As are the concealed comforts of a man
    locked up in a woman's love. . . .
I scent the air of blessings
When I come but near the house.
What a delicious breath marriage sends
    forth—
The violet bed's not sweeter.

Thomas Middleton

*L*ove does not consist in gazing at each other but in
looking outward together in the same direction.

Antoine de Saint-Exupéry

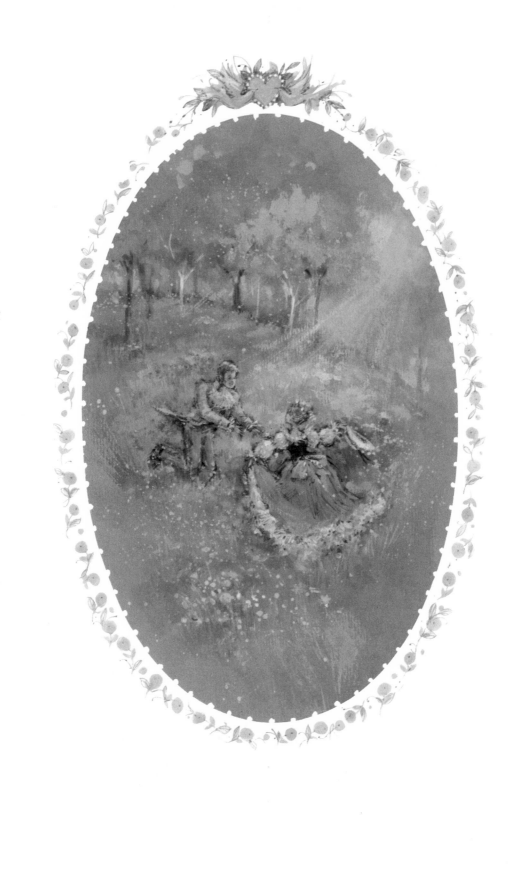

Men Marry What They Need.
I Marry You

Men marry what they need. I marry you,
morning by morning, day by day, night by night,
and every marriage makes this marriage new.

In the broken name of heaven, in the light
that shatters granite, by the spitting shore,
in air that leaps and wobbles like a kite,

I marry you from time and a great door
is shut and stays shut against wind, sea, stone,
sunburst, and heavenfall. And home once more

inside our walls of skin and struts of bone,
man-woman, woman-man, and each the other,
I marry you by all dark and all dawn

and have my laugh at death. Why should I bother
the flies about me? Let them buzz and do.
Men marry their queen, their daughter, or their mother

by hidden names, but that thin buzz whines through:
where reasons are no reason, cause is true.
Men marry what they need. I marry you.

John Ciardi

Marriage Is a Union

Marriage is not a federation of two sovereign states.
It is a union—domestic
                 social
                   spiritual
                     physical.
It is a fusion of two hearts—
   the union of two lives—
      the coming together of two tributaries,
which, after being joined in marriage, will flow in the same
   channel in the same direction . . .
carrying the same burdens of responsibility and obligation.

Peter Marshall

*B*lessed is the man that hath a virtuous wife,
for the number of his days shall be double. A
virtuous woman rejoiceth her husband, and he
shall fulfill the years of his life in peace.

Ecclesiasticus 26:1, 2

How Many Times Do I Love Thee?

How many times do I love thee, Dear?
Tell me how many thoughts there be
   In the atmosphere
    Of a new-fall'n year,
Whose white and sable hours appear
The latest flake of Eternity:—
So many times do I love thee, Dear.

How many times do I love again?
Tell me how many beads there are
   In a silver chain
    Of evening rain,
Unravelled from the tumbling main
And threading the eye of a yellow star:
So many times do I love again.

Thomas Lovell Beddoes

Doubt thou the stars are fire;
   Doubt that the sun doth move;
Doubt truth to be a liar;
   But never doubt I love.

William Shakespeare

A Soul-Stirring Marriage

You can see them alongside the shuffleboard courts
in Florida or on the porches of the old folks' homes
up north: an old man with snow-white hair, a little
hard of hearing, reading the newspaper through a
magnifying glass; an old woman in a shapeless dress,
her knuckles gnarled by arthritis, wearing sandals to
ease her aching arches. They are holding hands, and
in a little while they will totter off to take a
nap, and then she will cook supper, not a very good
supper, and they will watch television, until it is
time for bed. They may even have a good, soul-stirring
argument, just to prove that they still really care.
And through the night they will snore unabashedly, each
resting content because the other is there. They are
in love, they have always been in love, although sometimes
they would have denied it. And because they have been
in love they have survived everything that life could
throw at them, even their own failures.

Ernest Havemann

Two souls with but a single thought,
    Two hearts that beat as one.

Von Munch Bellinghausen

Unity

Heart of my heart, the world is young:
Love lies hidden in every rose,
Every song that the skylark sung
Once, we thought, must come to a close:
Now we know the spirit of song,
Song that is merged in the chant of the whole,
Hand in hand as we wander along,
What should we doubt of the years that roll?

Heart of my heart, we cannot die!
Love triumphant in flower and tree,
Every life that laughs at the sky
Tells us nothing can cease to be;
One, we are one with a song today,
One with the clover that scents the world,
One with the Unknown, far away,
One with the stars, when earth grows old.

Heart of my heart, we are one with the wind.
One with the clouds that are whirled o'er the lea,
One in many O broken and blind,
One as the waves are at one with the sea!
Ay! when life seems scattered apart,
Darkens, ends as a tale that is told,
One, we are one, O heart of my heart,
One, still one, while the world grows old.

Alfred Noyes

Set in Goudy Light Old Style, a delicately styled
original alphabet drawn by the American designer
Frederic W. Goudy for the Monotype in 1905.
Printed on Hallmark Eggshell Book paper.
Designed by Trudi M. Ludwig.